That's My Dog!

I HAVE A LABRADOR

T0805967

By Benjamin Proudfit

Gareth Stevens
PUBLISHING

Please visit our website, www.garethstevens.com. For a free color catalog of all our high-quality books, call toll free 1-800-542-2595 or fax 1-877-542-2596.

Library of Congress Cataloging-in-Publication Data
Names: Proudfit, Benjamin, author.
Title: I have a labrador / Benjamin Proudfit.
Description: Buffalo, New York : Gareth Stevens Publishing, [2026] | Series: That's my dog! | Includes index.
Identifiers: LCCN 2024034397 | ISBN 9781482469998 (library binding) | ISBN 9781482469981 (paperback) | ISBN 9781482470000 (ebook)
Subjects: LCSH: Labrador retriever–Juvenile literature. | Dogs–Juvenile literature. | Pets–Juvenile literature.
Classification: LCC SF429.L3 P76 2026 | DDC 636.752/7–dc23/eng/20240830
LC record available at https://lccn.loc.gov/2024034397

First Edition

Published in 2026 by
Gareth Stevens Publishing
2544 Clinton Street
Buffalo, NY 14224

Copyright © 2026 Gareth Stevens Publishing

Editor: Kristen Nelson
Designer: Leslie Taylor

Photo credits: Cover, p. 1 Chedko/Shutterstock.com; p. 5 Dimedrol68/Shutterstock.com; p. 7 claire norman/Shutterstock.com; p. 9 Annette Shaff/Shutterstock.com; p. 11 Natalia Fedosova/Shutterstock.com; pp. 13, 24 chrisukphoto/Shutterstock.com; p. 15 Brad Covington/iStockphoto.com; p. 17 Gajus/iStockphoto.com; p. 19 JennyMac Travel/Shutterstock.com; pp. 21, 24 Oskari Porkka/Shutterstock.com; p. 23 Iuliia Bondarenko/Shutterstock.com.

All rights reserved. No part of this book may be reproduced in any form without permission in writing from the publisher, except by a reviewer.

Printed in China

Some of the images in this book illustrate individuals who are models. The depictions do not imply actual situations or events.

CPSIA compliance information: Batch #QS26GS: For further information contact Gareth Stevens, New York, New York at 1-800-542-2595.

Find us on

Contents

This is my Labrador!
His name is Pete.
He is black.
He has brown eyes.

Pete's brother is yellow.
His sister is brown.

Pete loves to swim!
He has webbed toes.
These help him
swim well.

Labs need a lot of playtime.

Pete plays fetch.
I throw the ball.
He brings it back.

My dad and I take
him for long walks.

Labs are smart.
We took Pete to a
training class.
He learned quickly!

Labs like Pete grow big! They have strong bodies.

I take care of Pete.
I brush him.
He sheds sometimes.
This means he
loses his fur.

Pete is the best dog.
I love my Labrador!

Words to Know

fetch

shed

Index